"22 masterfully crafted narrative poems connote a poetic memoir that seizes the reader by his throat. It is hard to swallow all this despair, but you do. You immediately respect the resilience of the speaker, just as you respect and lavish the deft precision of each line. Despair breeds an all-too familiar gut punch in "Resurrecting Onions," a poem sharing the book's title. The poem is about a father/son Cub Scout planting project that, amid harsh conditions, manifests a plethora of onions. Ironically, its ninth stanza reads "Mom smothered / your damn liver / in them. / I never got to try one / before they shriveled / and dried /" While the speaker initially hints at marveling over a Cub Scout project serving as a catalyst to bud a relationship between father and son, the father kills it in the tenth stanza: "When the weather broke, / so did your patience / for the odor / of decomposing onions. /" Here the father forces the onions to be thrown away, but instead, the speaker reburies them. Borders is highly perceptive choosing the verb resurrecting in his title. The father abandons the son and family, and the poem concludes, "Like so much / they flourished / in your absence. /" Indeed. This book affirms Borders' prophetic line. Once you open it, you commit to enrichment. Reading this book will make you a better person, or in the very least, strengthen your resolve to be a better one."

—Sandra Feen, Evidence of *Starving* (Voice Lux Journal, 2021); *Meat and Bone* (Luchador Press, 2019); and *Fragile Capacities: School Poems* (Nightballet Press, 2018)

"From the opening stanza of the opening poem, *Resurrecting Onions* gives the reader a knee-buckling emotional uppercut. And then things get really brutal. This collection of autobiographical poems is a remarkable, and often heartbreaking, recounting of a childhood lost amid a father's violence and abuse. In recounting his experiences, James writes with a vividness and authenticity that makes the reader grateful for their own broken childhood. This collection serves as a cautionary tale of the shame that flows from a fractured family environment and the scars that follow one into adulthood. Fortunately, *Resurrecting Onions* also mirrors the author's life - a bleak beginning eventually turns triumphant by reminding us that it is possible to not only acknowledge, but positively harness, painful emotional experiences. And we are left with the hope - perhaps even a promise - that the cycle of generational dysfunction can be broken. Readers of James' collection are certainly in for a heavyweight emotional fight."

—Christopher Minton, Poet Laureate of Windrow Court

"In *Resurrecting Onions,* James Borders takes the reader on his hazardous journey from physical and emotional abuse toward finding a better life. He observes, "My mother and father ride side by side down / the city avenue…. She is / divorced from him. / He is dead." ("A Dream of Me") In poems, by turn intuitive, witty, and generous, he finds the strength to overcome a painful past and to learn to give and receive love. Struggle, wit, intuition, and generous spirit make this book one to read and reread. I don't often reread a book, but I read *Resurrecting Onions* four times!"

—Kathleen S. Burgess, *What Burden Do Those Trains Bear Away*

Resurrecting Onions

Poems by James Borders

Kung Fu Treachery Press

Rancho Cucamonga, CA

Copyright © James Borders, 2022

First Edition: 1 3 5 7 9 10 8 6 4 2

ISBN: 978-1-958182-12-3

LCCN: 2022940187

Author photo: Alyssa Borders

Cover image: Ralph Pratt, courtesy of the Leeds Museums and Gallaries.

Acknowledgments:

Grateful acknowledgement is made to *Madness Muse Press* in which "A Dream of Me" first appeared.

Special thanks to my friends and fellow poets Kathleen Burgess and Nik Macioci for graciously accepting the task of editing this book and pointing out all my ~~bad~~ poor grammar.

TABLE OF CONTENTS

FOREWORD

A raucous noise in halls of Linden-McKinley High School at this time of year meant doors had opened for an onslaught of students after summer break. Twenty-five headed for my room where I waited to teach them ninth-grade English. James Borders was among the twenty-five. He did not stand out for any special reason. Several days later; however, his witty remarks and humorous comments interrupted my lectures. What to do with a very bright student who wouldn't be quiet? My solution was to move his desk next to mine. As the year progressed, it became clear James was the brightest and most gifted student in the class.

During his junior year, he was a student in American Studies, a combination of history and English, a team-taught class. The history teacher often sat him in the hallway because he made comments and talked aloud. He didn't belong in a public school. He should have been in a special setting where there were teachers who could nurture his talent and very sharp mind. Only later did I learn he had suffered abuse as a child.

After his graduation, we went in separate directions. During that time, I learned later, he had tried to find me. It wasn't until I joined Facebook that we reconnected thirty years later. Since then, we have become very close friends.

James wrote well in high school, but now his work has elevated to a greater level of excellence. He told me I had been his surrogate father during those early years. Ironically, it was his father about whom he was reluctant to write. I pointed out the wealth of possibilities if he tapped into that subject. After many discussions, he did, and the result is *Resurrecting Onions*, an incredibly successful group of poems. It depicts his relationship with his father as well as the general dysfunctional background in which that relationship took place.

The opening poem establishes theme and mood. "I'm the bastard son, born out of wedlock, an uninvited / guest." It is true when he says, "torment and hatred still cling to me." What exactly did he think of his dad? He was "raising hell instead of a family." His father perpetrated much violence: "Fingers push against my face in a half fist." When six years old, his dad "forcefully shoves vileness into my mouth / fills my nasal cavity / with the foulest of food." His mother comes to his rescue, begs the dad "to let it go," but her plea doesn't keep the memory from casting a shadow over James' childhood and, in fact, his life. Violence continued into high school. "In my freshman year / I take my first beating / I take a full-on frontal attack by fist." James skipped school the next day; in fact, began to skip school regularly. Ironically, in the midst of violence, he plants a vegetable garden, something he can care for the way he wasn't.

Primarily narrative, poems in this collection are suffused with appropriate and fresh images that are compelling. *Resurrecting Onions* is laden with brutal truth, a brilliantly conceived journey through a troubled landscape. Despite the subject, this book leaves the reader uplifted and filled with satisfaction that the author chose, not a life of delinquency, but one in which he writes masterful poetry.

-R. Nikolas Macioci, Ph.D, Author of
Why Dance? and *Dark Guitar*
Groveport, Ohio 2022

For Nik, my teacher, mentor, critic, editor, and dear friend who asked constantly if I was done with this collection. I would not have had the courage to complete it without your unwavering support.

For my children, Grace and Mitchell, who I love so very much. May this book give insight into the dark places I often dwelled. Remember the good times and learn from the bad.

Plant your garden.
Grow your life.
If it starts to stink,
let it be the onions.

Resurrecting Onions

THE BASTARD SON

I am the bastard son, born out of wedlock,
an uninvited guest at my parent's wedding.
I am a shiny new toy, discarded
when the novelty wears off, to be abandoned
by a father at ten years old.

I am ten years a bastard. Mom struggles
to make sense of it, assures me I am not to blame,
that I am loved. I hear her weep alone.
I wish for her not to be sad. I beg for her
to be angry. I pray that we could both
find a way to move past the hurt.
Resentment answers my prayers.

I am fifteen years a bastard. I try to please,
make an effort to have praise placed upon me.
I am a disappointment, too cerebral, not a normal boy.
I can't play football, fix a car, get in fights.
Acceptance is only for his pleasure,
for his bragging rights. Look what *he* has done,
his son is smart and talented.
His self-pride frames the photo of my accomplishments.

I am twenty-four years a bastard. No longer am I
enchanted with the prospect of having a father.
I am a father, doting, devoted, determined not to make
the same mistakes that were thrust upon me.
Yet, a grandfather tries to redeem himself, wedges into a
family, oversteps, intrudes, insinuates himself. He crosses a
line so deeply drawn, he turns, rubs it out with a dusty boot.

I am twenty-six years a bastard. Distanced, removed,
exiled, a petty man threatens. Ignorance and peace are
devastatingly destroyed. No man can withstand the
damaging blow delivered
through a simple, callous, hateful phone call.
Truths are forced upon a family. Broken trust
is a betrayal not to be recovered.

I am forty-seven years a bastard. The crying is over.
Torment and hatred still cling to me, a constant cut
that stings and festers. I must abandon all
that reminds me, walk away from the dream
I clung to for a lifetime. I must move out
of the shadow of self-pity.

I am no longer the bastard. I'm told they boxed up
the misery that tortured me. They put dirt on an old
wound and buried it six feet. The scars he caused will
always be a constant memorial to a cancer
that spread over a lifetime. To reconcile his death
means to reconcile my life.
Today, it is made easier as the bastard
is laid to rest.

DESERTER

A convenient family,
a child bride cradles
a baby swaddled
in exemptive cotton.

Boys thrust into war,
men before their time.
You hide behind the
technicality of certificates.

Stay behind. Fight
the battles at home.
Protect and serve
widows and orphans.

You dodged them as well.

Vietnam is a far away
conflict, strife with moral
ambiguity. At home,
you have no ambiguity, no morals.

Raising Hell instead of a family,
you fight a war of turf conflict.
Your uniform: dirty Levi's, black
leather adorned with patches of anarchy.

Mustn't your mother be proud.

Much like Vietnam, the war
at home ended without resolution,
the death count yet to be determined.

RUSSELL JOHNSON

A man I never met fills me with questions,
makes me hopeful that an ugly truth
could erase doubt in myself.

Most men my age hear the name
Russell Johnson and think of the professor
on Gilligan's Island. I do not.

On the occasions my father was spiteful,
hateful, and petty, he would tell me
Russell Johnson was my father,
comments made to hurt me
and throw insults at my mother,
who has collected them
in a cedar chest beneath
old valentines and a worn leather
jacket, memories left to rot.

I was not the heir apparent to the scientist
on the deserted island, but of a man who lived
just blocks away from my own home.

My father denies me, puts uncertainty
in my head, makes me insecure, yet feel
the promise of a different outcome.
I harbor thoughts it could be true.

Mom assures me there is nothing
to his accusations, wishes
she could tell me otherwise,
that the footsteps I am destined to follow
are merely a walk in a fantasy situation comedy.

Is it possible not to become the man
that so cruelly mocks my existence?

Oh, how I wish the professor were here
to help me off this island.

LIVER FAILURE

His hand smashes into my face.
Motor oil stained, nails bitten
past the skin of the tips, his fingers
push across my face in a half fist.

This would be the first memory of violence
perpetrated against me. The hostile act
forever imprinted on my brain. To this day,
the smell of beef liver triggers
an automatic gag reflex,
and fear,
and anger.

Tears run down liver-crusted cheeks.
Heaving snot bubbles swell
and deflate with every stuttering gasp of air.

My childhood sense of security destroyed.
The man I look up to,
respect and revere,
forcefully shoves vileness into my mouth,
fills my nasal cavity
with the foulest of foods.
He would not be satisfied
until I ate the iron-heavy chunk of meat.

My mother begs him
to let it go, a plea that would resonate
throughout my childhood and,
to an extent, my life.

Red faced and cursing,
spittle flying from his foul-breathed mouth,
he continues his attack,
desiring the satisfaction
of controlling a six-year-old.

This will be the day I learn to stand my ground,
that I control my life.
It will lend the courage needed
for many more instances of violence against me.

In my freshman year of high school
I take my first beating.
There is no swat on the butt,
no leather belt wrapping around legs,
welts rising hot across my skin,
not even so much as a slap
about my body. This day
I take a full-on frontal attack by fist.

This man who towers over me,
an easy hundred pounds on me,
pummels me with ham hock like fists.

Did I deserve it? Maybe.
I'd been warned multiple times
about skipping school.

My father, fully satisfied
he has proven his control
over me, leaves me
with a warning of more to come
if I don't learn to listen.

I skip the next day of school.
My beat-down came and went,
the only bruises residing in my psyche.

Well into adulthood,
having a child of my own,
I once again become the target
of his rage. When confronted
with his false indignation,
I do not cower,
I do not flinch.

There is no longer a plea from mom.
She is long enjoying her escape.
There is only control.
At the poke of his finger
it is as if the power transferred
to me. I pack up my life
and move out of his.

I saw him for the first time
in twenty-two years,
a visit to a hospital to release myself
of residual control
he had over my life.
The room dark,

lit only by the dials and displays
of the machines keeping him alive.
He looked small.
The hepatitis, ironically,
takes control over him.

He does not need to be awake
for what I need to do.

The Bible commands
that I forgive him.
I told him as much,
that it is now between him and God.
When I leave, there is no sense of relief,
no weight lifted from me,
just a sense of self-loathing.

Two days later,
a request filtered through
to me to return
now that he was alert
and able to speak to me.
I realize,
be it ever so little,
that I now have the power,
over him,
and over myself.

VOICES

I performed routines
to entertain a drugged audience
of washouts and assholes.

My father would march me
out in front of his friends,
tell me to do those funny voices.

They would laugh, throw a wrench
at me and tell me to fuck off.
They are all dead now.

Impersonations came naturally.
I loved being someone else,
somewhere else.

I would mimic sounds as well—
a creaking door, barking dogs,
an old Nash Rambler.

My father would hear me
practicing behind closed doors.
Criticism always came.

*The world already has
one Jimmy Stewart.
It doesn't need another.*

Approval and support were as fleeting
as my prepubescent range.
I struggled to find a voice he would accept.

That didn't stop the exploitation
of my talent, or the abuse.
For him, the show must go on.

For my final performance
I opened the door, loaded the dogs,
and drove the Rambler far away.

RESURRECTING ONIONS

A Cub Scout requirement,
a father/son project:
plant a garden.
You laughed. Admittedly,
the odds were against me.

A cityscape,
no grass grew
in the backyard.
Rocks and tree roots
were the only crops.

Corn, pea, tomato seeds,
onion sets in a brown paper bag
bought from the local
hardware store with change
earned from a month
of collecting discarded
Coke and Pepsi bottles.

I tilled soil
with a tree branch
and an old, broken snow shovel.

Tender shoots scorched
by late August sun;
a late sowing, harsh conditions,
the corn tassel-free.

But the onions, oh
how they grew.

Like giant redwoods,
they stood tall
in shadows
of the apartment building
behind our house.

Winter came early
that year in Columbus, Ohio.
A bitter cold left frost
on green stems.
Their bright growth sparkled
beneath icy encasement.
Frost kills dreams.

I harvested, cleaned dirt
from my bountiful crop
of sweet, papery onions,
stored them in the coolness
of the dark basement.

Mom smothered
your damn liver
in them.
I never got to try one
before they shriveled
and dried.

When the weather broke,
so did your patience

for the odor
of decomposing onions.

You made me throw them out,
a half bushel of withered
vegetation in a dusty milk crate.
I reburied them
in a trench in the garden.

You were gone,
your precious boots
and jacket,
your box of priorities,
packed and moved
before the first sprout
of spring onions appeared.
Like so much,
they flourished
in your absence.

INHERITANCE

I'm not leaving my children shit.
They don't deserve anything I have.

I was the sole heir
to my father's legacy,
recipient of racist rants
like hand-me-down
Hummel figures, or his
coveted Reggie Jackson fly ball,
scrubbed clean of pine tar,
displayed in an acrylic case
lined in black velvet.

I am executor of abuse,
documented and notarized
by a record of torment
and pain, posted publicly
like the proclamation
of a tyrannical king.

I fought his will in probate,
wanting to return the putrid gift
of hate. It was like stacking drops
of water.

My children should inherit
more than that, enjoy
the generosity of my miserliness.
I wish my father hadn't left me shit.

A DREAM OF ME

My mother and father ride side by side
down the city avenue. Streetlights flicker
and pop as the car passes sad, neglected homes.
She is divorced from him.

He is dead.
What brings this unlikely family together?
My father hurls verbal abuse
from the front seat. I snatch it from the air

in an ongoing game of catch.
The car door flings open, I walk away
down backroads and alleys, searching
for the way home.

A black man guides me, loses me
in a perpetual loop of store fronts and backyards.
I tap tap tap my cell phone,
make attempts at reaching the living.

A white man pinches my ass,
his toothless grin tells me
he knows the way.
The damn phone cycles a circle of futility.

Dry heat and blurred houses oppress.
Incessant white noise drowns
pleas for help. tap Tap TAP!
The damn phone won't work.

Down the corridor, down the stairs,
running up to the basement, step
after growing step, climbing higher,
plunging deeper into darkness.

Back outside, the car blasts past me,
laughter howls from the radio
through a tin can speaker.
It's the damn phone.

Why won't it work?
Why can't anyone hear me?
Street people converge, pulling and pushing,
offering safety in their hugs.

An Uber driver named Destiny hurries
me into the back seat
of a long, white hearse. A black daisy wilts
over a bud vase on the dash.

She loads my baggage,
breaks the handle on my grip.
The car speeds away, leaving stars
in the exhaust. The laughter restarts.

My mom and dad ride
side by side.
She is still divorced from him.
He is still dead.

YEAH, THAT ONE

I had that dream again. You know the one
I'm talking about.
The one where my world is falling,
never seems to hit bottom.
The one where your wooly, gray face looks
in mine, like death trying to smile,
tells me everything is all right.
The one where you ignite the gaslight,
illuminate the path you want me to travel.
The dream cloaked in a shroud of lies
that hangs fashionably from your shoulders.
The dream I thought was over. Yeah, that one.

I had that memory again. You know the one
I'm talking about.
The one where my life spun out of control
like a broken wheel thrown loose from a car.
The one where your crystal-clear face looked defiantly
into mine and told me what I had already suspected.
The memory that saw tears wash over me
and soak into my essence.
The one that forever changed everything
about us, about me.
The memory I never wanted. Yeah, that one.

I had that suspicion again. You know the one
I'm talking about.
The one where my trust in people, people I loved,
who could never hurt me, left me and never returned.

The one where you avoided my face
when you nervously laughed, told me how crazy
the thought was.
The suspicion that made me doubt my own sanity, my
intelligence, my devotion to us.
The one that couldn't possibly be true.
Suspicion I should never have had. Yeah, that one.

I had that feeling again. You know the one
I'm talking about.
The one where my heart flip-flopped like a toddler
on a hot summer day.
The one where you gazed into my face, and I knew
for the rest of time I would feel joy.
The feeling that made me give openly everything
that was me.
The one that was not to be realized by a poor boy
from the Short North.
The feeling I should never deserve. Yeah, that one.

I had that loneliness again. You know the one
I'm talking about.
The one where I was content, if not happy.
The one where nobody lied to my face.
The loneliness that was bearable, uncomplicated.
The one that was enough.
The loneliness that I miss. Yeah, that one.

WHAT I COULD HAVE HAD

Her missing body startles me awake,
the sheets loose as if someone had pulled
my security blanket from clenched hands,
untucked my chin, left me vulnerable.

I creep down the stairs, leaving
my naivete behind, my suspicion pushed
out in front of me like a baseball bat,
protection from the truth to come.

Electric-blue light wavers beneath the door.
The clicks of a keyboard pounds out a familiar tune
like an out-of-control metronome.
A muted sigh, a smothered giggle escapes.

My wife ignores my warnings
of a co-worker's ulterior motives.
Or delights in them. Three o'clock in the morning
is not the time to find out which.

She gaslights me, tells me that I am paranoid
and ridiculous. I have heard this before.
I will not believe it this time. There is too much
dirty laundry heaped in my memory.

I tell her the man is looking for more
than she should be offering. She has already
given it away to too many. Again, she tries
to deflate my intensifying distrust.

As if in an old V-8 commercial,
I give her a soft hand to the back of her head,
try to make her realize, tell her to
wake up!

I sleep alone the rest of the night, sheets
wrapped mummy tight. She seeks a sympathetic ear
in her meddlesome girlfriend, taking the kids
with her for emphasis.

It would not be until mid-morning that police come,
escort me to NetCare: psychiatric intake.
After a thorough interview, a confused doctor
sends me home in a cab.

I am proud of my clean bill of mental health,
revel in my small victory, but the house is empty,
the monitor lights off to black, sheets bunched
where I had left them.

I telephone to inform her I am home,
anger builds with each button tone.
She is evasive, secretive, hostile,
if not outright rude, filled with her own denial.

I will be alone for the night. I survey
the vast emptiness of my self-respect. How had I
allowed this to happen again? I mentally slam
my hand onto my forehead in my own realization

of what I could have had.

RELUCTANT IMPRISONERS

The knock on the door was much softer
than I had witnessed on TV. No testosterone-fueled
cops with balled fists shouting *Police! Open up.*

No cautionary stand to the side of the door,
weapons drawn. The nine-light panel
like a two-sided, transparent tic-tac-toe board,

revealed two young women like uniformed girls
selling cookies for their troop. Again, the gentle rap
on the glass, only slightly more forceful.

I had been preparing for bed, alone in the solitude
of the over-dramatization of a cheating wife,
justification of actions that earlier had sent me
for a psych evaluation.

Sir, we have a warrant for your arrest.
We discussed particulars while I put my still warm shoes on.
Minds shook like bobble heads, disbelief in ceramic eyes.

Dignity afforded as they led me uncuffed
to the patrol car, left shackle free in the back seat.
Pleasant, apologetic conversation on the ride downtown.

Their glances revealed snapshots of sympathy
in the rear-view mirror, emotions of understanding
and frustration, carriers of justice in an unjust world.

Exiting the car outside the courthouse, ominous,
the color of skull, they fitted the required restraint,
one-click loose. Patted me on the shoulder, reassured.

Hole-and-corner conversation, the booking officer
double takes me on the plastic bench. Wishes of
good luck vanish into the background of
clanging cells and resignation.

PIG LATIN

I watch a muted television through steel bars,
a hefty blue-shirted pitchman pantomimes
the benefits of a soap powder. I absently smell
the frayed edge of the stiff, wool blanket
that covers my shivering body, realizing
it has been a while since it saw a wash of any kind.
Nevertheless, I keep it tucked under my chin

like the comforting hug from a grandmother.
I am beyond nervous, recall every story
I've ever heard about being in jail. My cellmates snore
lightly in bunks as I reflect on my situation and prepare
to defend my life with wit and good nature.
My consciousness slides away with the hours.
I am lulled to sleep by the glow of a knife

salesman on the screen.
Awakened by the indecipherable chitter
of my new roommates, my nerves jolt me
to an upright sitting position
as I take in the men in morning fluorescence.
There are no tattooed bikers, muscle-bound thugs
shaping shivs from plastic spoons.

A collection of every-man bodies stir
in metal cots like a group of kids
in a summer camp cabin. The foul stench

of stale yawns begins to envelope
the sleeping area as these would-be tough guys
wipe crust from eyes, drool
from corners of mouths.
They recognize the "fresh fish" look of panic
on my face, begin to welcome me to their
neighborhood. Thankfully, no one asks
why I am here. I know why I am here,
even if it doesn't make sense to me, wonder
how my situation compares to their crimes.
A Hispanic man speaks fractured English,

chats his plight while I try to avoid mine.
He asks if I speak Spanish.
Though I am sure that I remember enough
from middle school Spanish class
to tell him I can throw *lápiz por la ventana*
(pencil through the window), I tell him I do not.
He begs of me to give him any sense of home.

I access my memory bank and it comes to me.
I proudly spirit *el puerco rosado!*
He doubles over with laughter, advises me
not to use that phrase in jail. I feel the words
are innocuous enough since I had read them
on a bag of barbeque pork rinds. Laughing
even harder he translates the phrase to me saying

*Amigo, you will not make friends on the other side
of the bars. These words you say do not mean what
you may think. They mean "the pink pig".*

As we giggle like schoolboys in health class,
an overweight police officer comes, takes me away.
As the jail keep's keys rattle,
I take my new acquaintance's advice
under serious consideration.

BRANDED

You branded her with ink
and needles, saving the red-
hot iron to press and sear
into my memory.

The tattoo impressively
appropriate, a scarlet apple,
a mark that would make
Hester Prynne envious
of such fashionable betrayal.

A worm snakes out,
slithering deceit
from the forbidden fruit.
It's almost as if you both understand
metaphors, which you do not.

The permanence foreshadows
the beginning of the end,
as if the image were the cover
of a poorly written book
filled with chapters of lies.

She would try to rewrite
the ending, cover the tattoo,
make you nothing but a footnote.
Again, she was ignorant
in her awareness of metaphors,
choosing a heart with wings,
foreshadowing the last chapter.

BLACKMAIL

No ransom note, little chips of paper
cut and glued, spelling out demands
that could never be fulfilled.

Secret negotiations, deals manufactured
on the back of infidelity and deceit,
threaten blissful ignorance.

My father uses his own betrayal
as a tool to take away my child,
leaves little choice for his co-conspirator.

Revelation packed into baggage,
dropped in confessional heaps
upon the victim in heavy truths.

Hurt and anger are the price I pay,
details of betrayal perpetrated against me,
unshakable memories greater than loss.

LONGSHOT

The trigger is as cold as heartbreak,

the barrel, long and black as loss.
I sit in the swivel chair, moving back
and forth like a roulette wheel stuck
on an unlucky number, seeing only red.

The stock nuzzles into my shoulder,
the wood smooth against my cheek.
I picture my target, invisible, looming
like a thousand ghosts.

My father has refused me retribution, being content
with torment from afar, denying me
the satisfaction of his guilt and shame.
Or, perhaps, he has no feelings of remorse.

I turn the shotgun in my hand,
measure the possibility of reaching the trigger.
Surely, someone must die tonight.
I spin again and hope that it all goes to black.

WHAT DREAMS DO DARE– in Fibonacci

You
Came
To me
In a dream.
I had begged to sleep.
To be awake would be surreal.

Wickedness cannot but penetrate a conscious mind.

Shadows pass beneath eyelids, tormenters in darkness,
a vibrant wraith envelopes me.

Torrents of perspiration run mountain-stream-cold through
Egyptian cotton and puddle in an oasis of singular
enlightenment.

Pulse quickens, breathing hastens in thick pockets of warm
air while brightness fills the room, my blinded mind coerces
shadows into retreat, smudging them along the wall and
escaping beneath the doorway and leaves me to my dream.

ASUNDER

I
Them

A blasphemous tryst wrecks
the unstable foundation
of a marriage, kills
a relationship between father and son.
Betrayal drips thick
from forks at the dinner table.

Both, sworn to love, protect,
throw it all away
for carnal pleasure.

What God has brought together,
let no man bring asunder.

Cheap,
one-story motels,
newly painted room numbers.
Rates by the hour.
Parking lot rendezvous
in the shadows.
Shared secrets
among family.

II
Him

You never wanted me.
I was an inconvenient reminder
of your mistakes,
your own unhappy life.

Nothing I did
was good enough for you.
The things that came close
were met with jealousy.
What I had, you wanted.
You plotted to take it away.

Beneath your failures and insecurities,
criticism spewed from your mouth,
finding fault to assign.
You were supposed to care
for me unconditionally, protect me
from evils of the world.
Little did I know
you were evil personified.

When I escaped your grasp,
you shattered everything
that I lived for.

I cut you from my life
like a cancerous lesion.
It was liberating.

I sighed in relief
the day they told me you died.
It was about time.

III
Her

You bitch!
How dare you
prove everyone right.
Damn you
for breaking my heart,
making prophecy
of whispered rumors
by everyone I knew.

He called you a slut
when he first met you.
I defended you
for the better part of my life.
Both of you were determined
to prove him correct
and humiliate me.

The most intriguing
is how you blamed me.
I will accept responsibility
for many of the mistakes
in our marriage,
but I will not be made guilty
for you sleeping with my father.
I raise my glass to you,
relish the misery
you have caused yourself.

IV
Me

My life has been stolen
like a rare coin collection,
pennies at a time,
an album of empty pages,
faint impressions,
memories lost.

I doubted my instincts,
compromised my dignity.
I wore shame and embarrassment
like a prison jumpsuit.
I hid truth
in shadows of pity,
indignity and humiliation
veiled from everyone.

Sleepless nights,
dreams repeated
over and over
the nightmare I was living.
Whispers fed my suspicion.
Time and space lost
to post-traumatic blackouts.
Hate possessed me.

He is dead,
You are miserably alone,
living the life of your mother
you pitied for so long.

I am happy. A loving new wife,
wonderful children, grandchildren
surround me.

I no longer dream the dreams
that awakened me with deep sweats
and pounding heart. Now, I go to bed
with a clear conscience and in the morning
rise and thank God that you two found each other.

THE OLD HAUNT

I recently visited my childhood home.
Fresh coats of paint
could not hide deep scars
that still reside like grooves
in the wood frame of a closet door,
years of butter knives jammed in,
a makeshift lock hiding
Christmas presents from curious eyes.

The current tenant, or former,
as he was moving out, looked at me skeptically
from the sidewalk when I asked
to examine the old place.
I explained to him where we stood
was the very spot my sister was whisked away
to the emergency room
on Beggar's Night in 1977
after a cut lip from a neighbor's fence.

I showed him where the switch bush had loomed
like gallows in an old town square,
a passive aggressive deterrent,
that by the end of my teenage years
had been stripped bare.

I pointed out
the corner of the yard
where the onions had grown.

The man, now curious, if not sympathetic,
capitulated then acted as my tour guide
through a journey
of remembrance and regression.

The place seemed much smaller
than it had during my childhood
as I was able to reach the far side of the living room
in only a few steps. Beautifully mortared brick
was exposed on the fireplace.
I remember my father covering an unrecalled
surface with faux brick veneer.
It all seems so pointless now.

I ran my hand across rough, plastered walls,
recalled the smooth texture
of wood paneling that never stayed
securely attached to the lime and gypsum
blend that clung to nails in vain.
Instinctively, I reached to the top right
corner of the doorway and felt disappointment
when I did not find the old gas light outlet pipe.
I experienced much disappointment in that house.
Immediately, sophomoric thoughts
of those giant lead nipples
throughout the house flashed in my mind's eye,
then poked me blind.

We continued down my memory lane.
I point out where everything is in the wrong place.

The bathroom was no longer
on the opposite wall from the kitchen,
both having been added to the back of the home
years later when indoor plumbing had come into style.

The kitchen, no longer the confined quarters
that had been my own personal culinary school,
not out of interest but necessity, was now twice
as big, yet still thoroughly inadequate.
Gone was the giant one-compartment, cast-iron sink
under which I played by clanging Pepsi bottles
together while my mom warned me from above
to stop right up until the moment they broke and I
received my first visible wound in that house.

Bedrooms, once grand in size,
now partitioned and revived with life
of which I only dared dream.
A vibrant, modern, functional bathroom
was added to the upstairs, a hallway built
connecting all the rooms to it.
An awkward discomfort swept over me;
I stood in this stranger's bathroom,
or he in mine. Curiosity was piqued, a temptation
to take inventory of his medicine cabinet.

Silence befell me.
I would respect his memories
of his time here as much as
I would try to repress mine.

I thanked him, wished him luck in his move.
He thanked me for a history
that would no longer be of any consequence.

From the short hall, I stared
out at a depressing view from the picture window
that was no longer there but very much existed
inside of me, hesitated. As if reading my thoughts,
my guide asked me if I would like to look at the
basement. My mind raced, my heart beat faster,
I reached for the knob.

As the door swung toward us
I explained to him that in my final years at home
I had moved into the basement.
The man was awash with shock.
You slept in this basement?
I assured him I had and began my descent
into the abyss, shivered in the shadow of memories.
Maybe I was trying to punish myself
for having tried so hard to forget my origins
and having hid shame I felt for having lived there.

The steps were familiar and strong.
Gone were the two-by-four framed walls
that covered the moist block foundation.
Gone was the 8-track jukebox,
the velvet black-light poster
that reminded me daily to "Keep on Truckin.'"
Gone was the feeling of complete aloneness.

Anxiety built in me.
I turned toward the back side of the basement.
My stomach churned.
Goose flesh came over my body in waves.
There, in the farthest right corner of the basement
was the single greatest cause of nightmares
during my formative years.
There was the only darkness of my childhood
that I could escape,
and I was face-to-face with it again.
That god-damned coal room, dark,
dank, stood taunting me.
A chill ran up and down my spine.
I wanted to leave, disappear,
but the man had other plans.
He wanted to discuss the room.
He told me the room gave him quite the scare
and he avoided that corner at all costs.
My irrational fears were validated.
I saw in this man, a perfect stranger,
my younger self, vulnerable,
scared, and seemingly all alone.
I wanted to hug him but thought better.
As I left, I told him that I hoped he also
had some good memories
in the house and that, unlike me,
would never feel the need to return.

GRACE

"Child abuse casts a shadow
the length of a lifetime."
—Herbert Ward

I struck my child

multiple times,
open hand, closed fist.
I betrayed her trust
with the repugnant
notion that it was protecting her.

Daily, I wear the shame
like a suit of barbed wire,
stitched in guilt,
fastened with buttons
of regret.

She chose hardness,
struggle, a half-life.
Her decisions contrary
to all I fought
to shelter her from.

The damage frames
family portraits
of broken smiles,
hangs heavy on the wall
of a new generation
to bare the weight

of a parent's misguided love.
With every hug
from my little girl
and her little girls
the barbs push deeper,
slicing into my heart.

I pull them closer,
inviting the pain
I caused.

Forgiveness is not deserved.
If she were to offer anything,
all I would ask for is Grace.

THE LAST POEM

The last poem
was supposed to be
the last poem
about child abuse
in my family.

I changed the name
of the computer folder
to FINISHED.

Fate and Karma
indicated they were
not yet done.

I right click,
try to relabel
the next generation
of injustice.

THREE GIFTS

Three little gifts,
white elephant exchanges
from a tortured family
Christmas in July,
passed from relative to relative,
looking to find a home.

Their mother, both a victim
and suspect of abuse,
neglects the children
and agency responsible
for protecting them.

They are whisked away
in the unconsciousness of sleep,
taken to an overly concerned
grandmother.
She watches drama unfold
like a movie goer munching
on a bucket of popcorn, delighting
in audience participation.

After one week, reviews are in
on her own played-out rehash
of a tired remake.
Three thumbs down say the critics.

Blue and white lights animate
needles on midsummer pine.

Children once again whisked away
through the fog of dying innocence.

The uncle and aunt volunteer
to save these three mistreated, misplaced
misfits. Realization soon gives way
to regret. Barely twice the eldest's age
these well-meaning parents of a toddler
took on more than was fair to anyone.

Again, a move must be made.
This time, there is no fighting,
no cursing, no wig-wag lights.
The girls are allowed to calmly,
and with care, pack their belongings
and say goodbye.
A grandfather empties years
from spare bedrooms, dusty trinkets
of holiday exchanges past.

The oldest tries to manage the disruption,
tells the younger two to behave
and respect their mother's father.
This is the last place for us to go.
Grandpa doesn't have to take us in.
But she's wrong. I do. I want to.

I want to end the cycle
of the white elephant exchange.
I want to give a home
to the three little gifts.

RITUAL

The filter of the copse of winter-bare trees
falls to morning sun that touches the bare flesh
of my head. Bending slightly forward,
my back groaning with the movement, I reach

for my coffee, put the cup to my lips, feel the crust
of the previous day's morning cookie rough
on my cracked skin, my morning ritual,
the tallying of death, both current and yet to come.

I count orange paint splotches on ash, slump
at the number of diseased trees that will be culled,
cut up, stacked along the property line for firewood.
Chickens strut, twitch about in a strobe-like fashion

like tweaker birds looking for their next fix of grain.
The pleasantry of a quick game on my phone,
checking social media gives way to the necessity
of reviewing emails and bank account balances.

Steam of a silent sigh hangs, mixes with aromatics
of lightly creamed coffee. The stress of my last step
in a routine that starts each day with anxiety and despair
blows away the cloud of rising vapors.

The news app opens, wishes me good morning,
splashes electric news onto the liquid screen—
a fire in the South End, foibles of the president,
a treasured American actress has passed away—
all unwelcome news,

all entirely of no bearing on my life. I scroll, scan,
find the crime report, stare down the article about the dead
body of a woman found on the northeast side of Columbus,
my thumb, light over the article like a razor-sharp blade of a
guillotine held suspended.

I click, look for street names, identifications, circumstances.
Wrong area, wrong description. Relief overwhelms me. I stare
into the yard, recount the orange dots that plead with me to be
pardoned, survey the hens that have become nonproductive,
dependent, and say to myself, not today.

James Borders is a poet, husband, grandfather, and recovering curmudgeon. After decades of writing pithy satirical poems and grocery lists, he decided to get serious about poetry which has resulted in his first book, *Resurrecting Onions*. James is a member of Bistro Poetry and the host of Peripatetic Poets based in Columbus, Ohio. Recent poems have appeared in *Meniscus Literary Magazine* and *Madness Muse Press*. This book shares the poet's struggles in order to help others suffering abuse to know recovery and a better life is possible and can break the cycle of victimization. They do not deserve the gaslighting or the tearing down of one's self worth. When not writing poetry, James spends his time woodworking, gardening, napping, and trying to spend time with his wife, Evelyn, all while raising three granddaughters. You can reach him at JamesBordersPoetry@ Gmail.com